MW01224797

An Idea Becomes a Book

by Trish Marx
illustrated by Diane Greenseid

SCHOOL PUBLISHERS

Printed in Mexico

ISBN 10: 0-15-350286-X
ISBN 13: 978-0-15-350286-6

Ordering Options
ISBN 10: 0-15-349940-0 (Grade 5 ELL Collection)
ISBN 13: 978-0-15-349940-1 (Grade 5 ELL Collection)
ISBN 10: 0-15-357323-6 (package of 5)
ISBN 13: 978-0-15-357323-10 (package of 5)

1 2 3 4 5 6 7 8 9 10   126   12 11 10 09 08 07 06

When you are at the library or bookstore, do you ever wonder who writes all those books? Many different people write those books. Authors can be young people, older people, famous people, and some unknown people who become famous after they have written a book! Even you could write a book. We'll go through the steps of publishing a book. In the end, you will know how a book is published.

Every book starts with an idea. Authors can write about any subject that interests them. What kind of books do you like? Perhaps you like to read fiction books with stories that the author has made up. Perhaps you like to read nonfiction books with true stories about real things. If you like nonfiction books, maybe you can write about something that happened to you. Perhaps you could write a biography, a true story about another person. If you like fiction, maybe you could write a story full of adventure. Perhaps you like detective and mystery stories or fantasy stories about talking animals?

Also, think about the time period when the story takes place. You can write about something that happens in the past, present, or the future.

It is important to think about whether your story would interest other people, too. This is especially important if you want your story to become a book. People who make books are looking for stories that would interest readers.

A publisher is a company that turns the book from words on a piece of paper into a book. Publishing a book is expensive because many people work on it. Publishers usually publish books that the publishers think many people will buy. The publisher will lose money on a book that people don't buy.

You have written your story. Now you can make your own book by dividing your story into sections, one section for each page. Keep your reader turning those pages by making the last sentence on each page exciting or suspenseful. Don't forget to leave room for the illustrations, or pictures!

How would you like to illustrate your book? Take a look at your favorite books. Get an idea of the many ways books can be illustrated. You can illustrate your book with line drawings, watercolor paints, chalk, or bold construction paper cutouts. Maybe you want to use photographs. Ask an adult in your family whether you can use some photographs from your family album. Maybe you could cut out pictures from a magazine.

Now paste your drawings or photos on each page. Write in page numbers, chapter titles, and captions in fun colors and print. This is called designing your book. Publishers have book designers who are responsible for every detail of the book. Details include the color of ink used and how much white space is on each page.

There is one special page in most books called the dedication page. It usually is in the front of the book. The author thinks of someone special who has helped or inspired the author along the way. That special person's name is listed on the dedication page usually with thanks from the author. Dedicating a book to someone is like giving a person a medal. It is an honor to have a book dedicated to you.

Think about the person you'd like to honor with a dedication. Your parents? A brother or sister? A grandparent? A friend? Maybe a teacher? Perhaps your dog? Then think about something special to say and write it on that page.

Now you have your book. It's time for revisions. Ask a friend to read it. Tell your friend to be very honest with you. Is the main character interesting? Does your reader care about what happens to the main character? Is there a problem in the book? Who solves the problem? Readers usually like the characters to solve their own problems. Does the character grow and change?

If your book is nonfiction, have you checked all of your facts? Even if you have written a fiction story, some facts may need to be checked, too. Is the ending satisfying? Does it leave the reader with most of his or her questions answered?

Do you think you are ready to send off your book to a publisher? Some books at the bookstore or library can help you decide where to send your manuscript, or what you have written. These helpful books list many different publishers and the kind of books they are interested in publishing.

Send a copy of your manuscript to a publishing house. Include a cover letter telling who you are and why you wrote the book. An editor might read your manuscript. Sometimes editors send back rejection letters that say the book is not right for them. Other times they ask for changes. They give you a chance to send your manuscript to them again. Celebrate when an editor says "yes" to publishing your book!

The real work begins when the book is accepted by the publisher! Most likely your editor will ask you to make changes in your manuscript. Maybe it needs to be longer or shorter. Maybe the plot needs to be more interesting. Sometimes writers are asked to add or remove characters from the story. Sometimes an editor suggests more dialogue, or speaking. You can cut words and descriptions that will be shown in the illustrations if your book is a picture book. Remember, though, that it is your story. You should always make the final decision on changing the manuscript.

Next, the editor will send your book off to be printed. This is when you have to be very patient. Sometimes months pass before receiving the book back from the printer. It is worth waiting for, however. Holding a book with your words, or possibly your words and your illustrations, is very special. This is when you can sit in a comfortable chair and read your book from front to back cover. Then invite your friends to a party to celebrate!

Scaffolded Language Development

SIMPLE AND COMPOUND SENTENCES Write the following sentence on the board:

Writing a book can be lots of fun, but it can also be hard work.

Tell students that this sentence is a compound sentence. Compound sentences are made up of two simple sentences, connected by a conjunction such as *and* or *but*. Circle the connecting word *but* in the sentence. Then rewrite the sentence as two simple sentences:

Writing a book can be lots of fun. It can also be hard work.

Model talking about things in the classroom using compound sentences. Examples might include: *Sue has a pencil, and she is writing a story*; or *We made a mess, but we will clean it up.* Then have students read the following sets of simple sentences. Ask students to join the sentences together to make one compound sentence using *and* or *but*.

1. The writer had an idea. He didn't think the editor would like it.

2. Julie likes to write mysteries. She likes to read mysteries, too.

⭐ Language Arts

Book Outline Have students write an outline of an idea for a book. Ask them to discuss their outlines and why they chose the topic.

 ### School-Home Connection

Write a Book Have students share what they have learned about publishing a book with family members. Encourage them to discuss what topic they would choose if they were writing a book.

Word Count: 1,017